Save the Sea Otters!

T0363956

Written by Mary-Anne Creasy

Illustrated by Ian Forss

Flying Start
to Literacy®

Contents

Chapter 1

Looking for sea otters

Lee looked for sea otters every day.
She saw fishing boats and
lots of jet skis, but no sea otters.

Lee had done a project on sea otters at school. There hadn't been any sea otters in Maple Bay for 100 years and they were coming back. Lee wanted to be the first to see them.

Then, one day, Lee saw one. It was on the beach. *Something is wrong*, thought Lee. *It should be on the sea, floating on the kelp.*

Lee ran and told her dad.

"Are you sure it's a sea otter?" said Dad.

"Yes," said Lee.

Lee and her dad went down to the beach. The otter was breathing, but it couldn't move.

"It needs help," said Dad. And he called the ranger.

The ranger came quickly.

"It has a broken flipper," said the ranger. "That's why it can't move. We will have to take it to the animal hospital."

At the animal hospital, the vet looked at the sea otter.

"It looks like it was hit by a boat," said the vet.

"Or a jet ski?" said Lee. "I read that otters sleep on the kelp on top of the water. Maybe the jet skiers can't see them."

"Yes, it could have been a jet ski," said the vet.

"We will need to make the bay safe so that this doesn't happen again," said Lee.

Chapter 2

In the news

A reporter came to talk to Lee
and the ranger.

"Are the sea otters back in Maple Bay?"
asked the reporter.

"We've found one otter," said the ranger.
"Lee was the first person to see it."

"Can you tell me about the sea otter?"
the reporter asked Lee.

"It has a broken flipper," said Lee.
"I think a jet ski ran over it.
We have to stop the jet skis."

That night, Lee saw herself on TV. They showed her talking about stopping the jet skis.

But then they showed some people and they were angry. They didn't want to stop the jet skis.

Lee was worried. She hadn't meant to make people angry.

"There is a meeting at the town hall tomorrow night," said Dad.

"Can we go?" said Lee.

"Yes," said Dad. "Let's go and find out what's happening."

Chapter 3

Lee's solution

There were lots of people at the town hall.

"Now that the sea otters are coming back to Maple Bay, what can we do to help them?" said the town leader.

"We should ban the jet skis," said the ranger.

"I won't make any money if you ban the jet skis," shouted the owner of the jet ski shop.

"And people won't visit Maple Bay for their holiday," said the owner of the camping ground.

Lee had an idea. Slowly, she stood up.

"You could take people on your boat to watch the sea otters," she said.

Everyone looked at her.

"But people want to go on jet skis," said the owner of the jet ski shop.

"They could go to the next bay,"
said Lee. "There isn't any kelp there
and there won't be any sea otters."

"You're right!" said the town leader.
"Maybe we can look after the otters,
but not ban the jet skis."

Chapter 4

Back in the sea

The next week, the ranger met Lee down by the bay. He had a cage and inside the cage, was the sea otter. Its flipper was better.

"Today's the day, Lee," said the ranger.

Lee opened the cage and the sea otter went into the sea.

"You made the bay safe for this sea otter," said the ranger.

"I can't wait until there are lots of sea otters in Maple Bay," said Lee.

Every day, Lee watched the sea otter in the bay from her house.

And then one day, she saw her otter with some other otters. It was a family.

The sea otters had returned to Maple Bay!